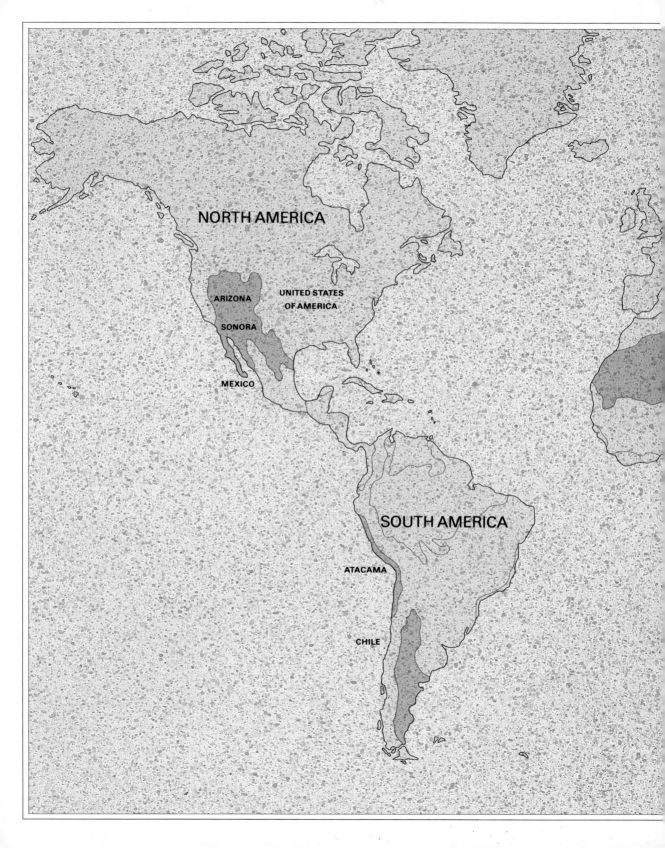

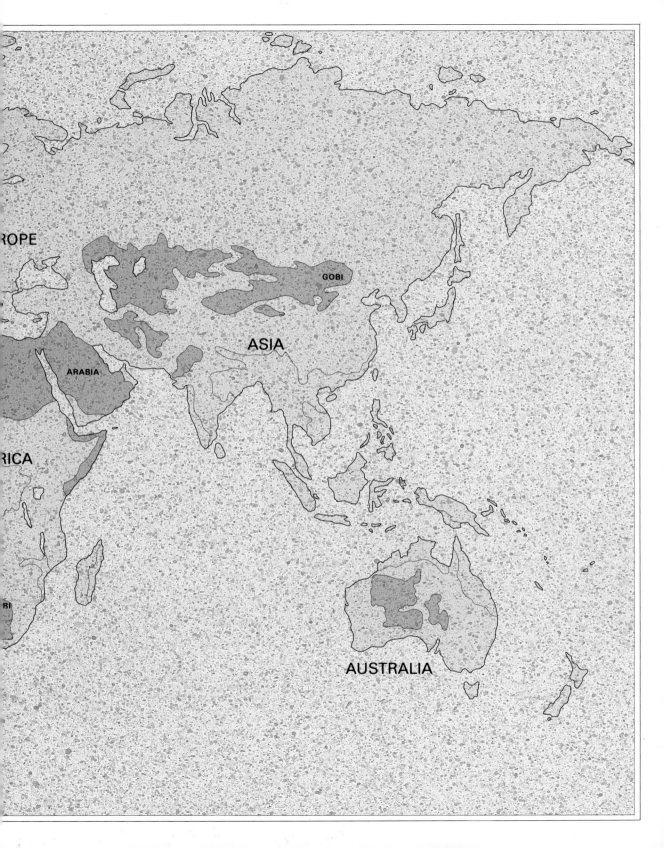

For Nicola   C.C.

For Sophie   B.McI.

First published in the United States 1984
by Dial Books for Young Readers.
A Division of Penguin Books USA Inc.
375 Hudson Street
New York, New York 10014
Published in Great Britain by Walker Books Ltd.
Text copyright © 1983 by Clive Catchpole
Pictures copyright © 1983 by Brian McIntyre
All rights reserved
Library of Congress Catalog Card Number: 83-7757
Printed in Hong Kong
First Pied Piper Printing 1985
A Pied Piper Book is a registered trademark
of Dial Books for Young Readers,
a division of Penguin Books USA Inc.
® TM 1,163,686 and ® TM 1,054,312
ISBN 0-8037-0037-7

THE LIVING WORLD
DESERTS

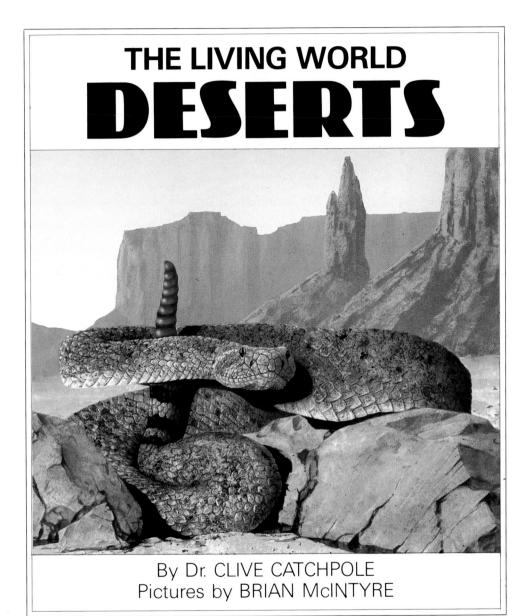

By Dr. CLIVE CATCHPOLE
Pictures by BRIAN McINTYRE

DIAL BOOKS FOR YOUNG READERS

Deserts are often thought of as vast expanses of sand—harsh, empty places baked dry by the searing sun. But not all deserts fit this description. Some lie in extremely cold parts of the world and have frigid climates, while even scorchingly hot deserts can become quite cool at night. Some deserts are rocky rather than covered with sand, and others have large areas of salt or ice. All deserts do have one thing in common, however—very little rain or water. They are dangerous places for living things, which need water to survive. Yet, despite this fact, even the hottest, driest desert can support a wonderful variety of plant and animal life.

Of all desert animals the camel may be the most extraordinary. The Arabian camel, or dromedary, can cross thirty miles of desert a day and has been known to go without water for seventeen days. When a thirsty camel reaches an oasis, it may consume as much as twenty-five gallons of water. This will be retained rather than lost through sweating. The camel does not need to sweat as a means to cool off—it can tolerate a body temperature of 106 degrees Fahrenheit. At night its temperature will drop as heat is lost to the cooler air. Camels can also go for days without food. Their large humps store fat, which accumulates after the camel has had plenty to eat. Then, when food is scarce, this reserve is drawn on.

Plants have also developed unique ways of surviving in the desert. Cacti have large, fleshy stems in which they store water and thick outer skins covered with wax that help prevent water loss. Needle-sharp spines protect the prickly pear cactus from hungry or thirsty desert animals such as the jackrabbit, which likes to rest in its shade.

The jumping cholla cactus of North America has spines so incredibly sharp that it is possible to be impaled by simply touching one. Yet the mourning dove is able to build her nest right in the middle of the thorns. She may be uncomfortable, but she is also much safer from predators.

The giant saguaro cactus is found in the Sonoran Desert of the United States and Mexico. It grows to almost fifty feet and is so big that it provides a home for many birds. The gilded flicker and other woodpeckers make nest holes in the fleshy stems. If their holes are abandoned, other birds such as the tiny elf owl will often move into them.

Desert bushes like the mesquite cannot store as much water as cacti. Instead, they have roots that can grow up to fifty feet long and tap water hidden deep underground.

Desert locusts are found in North Africa and Asia. In dry periods there are very few of them, but when it rains, more young survive because there is more vegetation to feed on. Thousands of young locusts will hop around together until, after three weeks, they become winged adults capable of flight. When food runs out, they will take off in swarms so large that they can blot out the light of the sun. The wind may sweep them to more fertile areas outside the desert, where millions can descend like a plague and strip bare whole areas of crops.

Life cycle of a locust

Mating

Egg-laying

Eggs

Hatchlings

Third-stage hopper   Fifth-stage hopper   Adult locust

Beetles are among the desert's most common insects. A thick outer covering prevents their bodies from losing water, and they remain cool by burrowing deep into the sand. In the desert nothing is wasted; the scarab beetle eats the droppings of camels and goats. It rolls the ball of dung into its underground chamber, where its young can also feed off it for many weeks. Scorpions hunt these beetles and other prey by hiding under rocks to ambush them. They kill with the poisonous stinger at the end of their tails. A sting from this North African scorpion can kill a person in four hours.

Snakes and lizards are both reptiles—
cold-blooded animals that thrive under the hot
desert sun. They get most of their water from
eating other animals, and their tough, scaly
skins help prevent water loss. Rattlesnakes
coil up to strike and kill rodents such as
kangaroo rats with a bite from their huge,
poisonous fangs. The rattle at the end of their
tails warns animals to keep away. Although
scales help snakes to grip and move over
rocky areas, sand dunes are a problem for
limbless animals. The sidewinder moves by
using its whole body to lever itself along.

Because lizards lie in the open under the desert sun and are easily visible to predators, they have developed special methods of protection. The Gila monster of the southwestern United States and Mexico has a poisonous bite—one of the only such lizards in the world with this trait. The Australian thorny devil is covered with sharp spines that make it almost impossible for another animal to eat it. The frilled lizard, also from Australia, has a very unusual technique: it stands up, opens its mouth wide, and unfolds an enormous frill. This makes it look much larger and more dangerous than it really is.

Unlike reptiles, mammals are warm-blooded animals with fur or hair and are much less tolerant of the desert heat. They often avoid it by resting in burrows during the day and then coming out at night to look for food. In this way their bodies save precious water because they do not sweat as much to keep cool. Desert rats such as jerboas don't drink at all but get the moisture they require from the seeds and roots they consume. In the Sahara, jerboas are hunted by the fennec fox, which also eats any insects it can find. Both the jerboa and the fennec stay cool by letting off body heat through their very large ears.

The sand grouse of Africa and Asia is one of the few birds that nests in the open, far from any water. Parents shade their eggs from the sun by sitting on them or standing above them. When the young hatch, the adults may fly over thirty miles each day to bring them fresh water. They soak their breast feathers and return; the young drink by passing the wet feathers through their beaks.

Vultures are a common sight in the desert. Soaring high on the hot currents of air, their sharp eyes search for signs of dead or dying animals to feed on. Because they have weak beaks and lack the strength of other birds of prey, they rarely attack animals that are not helpless.

Some deserts have rain at least once a year, and it is here that animals that normally exist only in water can be found. The spadefoot toad of North America uses its hind feet to bury itself almost completely beneath the sand, where it may wait for several months for the next rainfall. When small pools form, the toads quickly emerge, mate, and lay their eggs in the water. The tadpoles grow into adult toads in a few weeks—just in time to bury themselves before the pools dry out. The toads are able to feed on the thousands of desert shrimp eggs that have also hatched nearby.

For plants rooted in the dry desert sand, rain provides the opportunity to take in water, grow, and even flower. The sand is also full of seeds that will spring up as soon as the rains come. Because the water will not last, desert annuals such as sand verbena must germinate, grow, flower, and produce seeds in a very short time. These seeds will survive in the dry ground for months until the torrential showers return. Then the desert will bloom, suddenly becoming one of the most colorful and beautiful sights in nature.

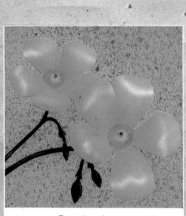

Parakeelya
Australia

Blue Gilia
U.S.A., Mexico

Añañuca Lily
Chile

Living Stone
South Africa

California Poppy
U.S.A., Mexico

Sturt's Desert Pea
Australia

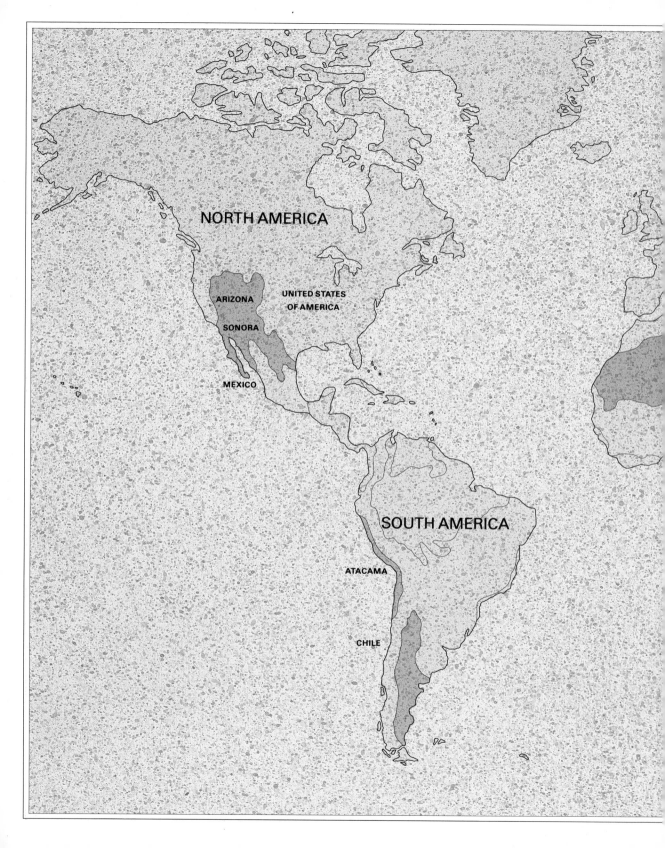